S0-BCN-608

Sharks!

by

Dorothy Francis

Perfection Learning®

Dedication

For Richard

About the Author

Dorothy Francis has written many books and stories for children and adults. She and her husband, Richard, divide their time between Marshalltown, Iowa, and Big Pine Key, Florida.

Ms. Francis holds a bachelor of music degree from the University of Kansas. She has traveled with an all-girl dance band, taught music in public and private schools, and served as a correspondence teacher for the Institute of Children's Literature in Connecticut.

As an environmentalist, her goal is to make her readers aware of the creatures around them and their need for nurturing and protection.

Ms. Francis has also written *Toy Deer of the Florida Keys* and *Sea Turtles: Creatures of Mystery*, which are part of the Animal Adventures series.

Cover Photo: Innerspace Visions/©Bob Cranston

Image Credits: Innerspace Visions/©Doug Perrine pp. 10 (top & bottom), 20, 21, 23, 42 (bottom), 44; Innerspace Visions/©Campbell/Womack p. 6; Innerspace Visions/©Jeff Rotman p. 12 (top); Innerspace Visions/©Masa Ushioda p. 17; Innerspace Visions/©Howard Hall p. 24; Innerspace Visions/©Ron & Valerie Taylor p. 32; Innerspace Visions/©Richard Herrmann p. 34 (bottom); InnerspaceVisions/©Phillip Colla p. 35; Innerspace Visions/©Mark Strickland p. 36

ArtToday (some images copyright www.arttoday.com); Corel Professional Photos pp. 5, 15 (top & bottom), 26, 27, 29, 30, 34 (top), 42 (top)

Text © 2001 Perfection Learning® Corporation.
All rights reserved. No part of this book may be used or reproduced in any manner whatsoever without written permission from the publisher.
Printed in the United States of America. For information, contact Perfection Learning® Corporation, 1000 North Second Avenue, P.O. Box 500, Logan, Iowa 51546-0500.
Tel: 1-800-831-4190 • Fax: 1-712-644-2392

Paperback ISBN 0-7891-5316-5
Cover Craft® ISBN 0-7807-9717-5
3 4 5 6 7 8 PP 08 07 06 05 04 03

CONTENTS

Chapter 1

The Invitation

Jack dressed to go shark fishing with his dad. He looked around his room. He glanced at his adopt-a-manatee certificate. It was in a frame on his desk. A picture of a dolphin hung above his bed. His sea turtle book lay nearby.

Jack was not looking forward to this fishing adventure.

Sharks eat almost any sea creature, Jack thought. His teacher had said so. Jack guessed they'd eat humans too—if they had the chance!

Jack had never seen *Save the Shark* bumper stickers. He had never heard good news about sharks.

And now Dad wanted to go shark fishing. Jack wanted to stay home.

Jack opened a desk drawer. He pulled out a scrapbook. He had been saving news clippings about sharks all summer. He read the headlines.

Shark Kills Boy in Surf

Caution: NO SWIMMING!

Sharks Sighted in Area

Shark Attack Suspected

Then Jack studied some of the pictures. He saw shoes, deer antlers, dog tags. All had been found in the stomach of one shark. It was scary stuff!

Jack was going to use the information when school started. He had signed up for a speech class. And he planned to scare his classmates with shark tales.

 8

Dad rapped on Jack's door and pushed it open. "Ready to go?"

"I feel rotten," Jack moaned. "Can we go another day?"

Dad smiled. "Getting cold feet?"

"Maybe a little bit," Jack muttered. He hated admitting he was afraid.

Dad saw Jack's clippings. "Sharks have a rotten **reputation**," he said. "But remember this. More people die from bee stings than from shark attacks."

Slowly, Jack followed his dad out of the house. He trudged to their dock.

"We'll head for some tidal **flats**," Dad said. "Water depth there is usually three or four feet. Maybe less. Sharks like the warm, shallow water."

"What kind of sharks will we see?" Jack asked.

"Can't say for sure," Dad said. "Scientists know of over 300 species."

 9

"But here in the Florida Keys we may see hammerheads," Dad continued. "Or bonnets. Nurse sharks are common here too."

hammerhead sharks

bonnet shark

nurse shark

"Exactly how big are they, Dad?" Jack asked.

"The average size is around five feet," Dad said. "Let's go see what we can find."

Jack took his time getting into the boat.

"Get a move on, Jack," Dad said. "The sun, wind, and tides are right. We'll have a good day on the flats."

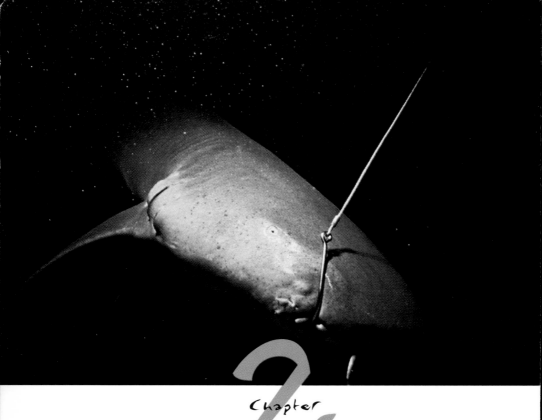

Chapter 2

Let's Catch a Shark

How small their boat seemed! It was just 16 feet long.

Jack remembered a shark movie he had seen. He remembered open jaws with razor-sharp teeth.

They had split a small boat in half. Jack shivered.

"Toss the line onto the dock," Dad said.

Jack released the line. He plopped onto the fishing chair and leaned back. The sun warmed him. He smelled **jasmine** on the **trade wind**.

Dad inched the boat through their **canal**. Once in the deep-water **channel**, Dad revved the motor. Jack tasted salty spray as they sped forward.

Dad sang "A Pirate's Life for Me." Jack's heart sang "Home, Sweet Home."

"Sharks are **ancient** creatures," Dad explained. "They lived on Earth before the dinosaurs. They're survivors. I have great respect for them."

Dad stopped the boat in waist-deep water. "Grab your rod, Jack. The bait's ready."

Slowly, Jack eased a pole from the rod case. He eyed the line. Then he touched the hot-pink tube at the end. Hooks poked through the tube.

 13

"This is the bait?" Jack asked. "This won't work. Sharks only like bloody flesh."

"Splash the tube around on top of the water," Dad said. "Sharks react to disturbed water."

Jack relaxed. No shark will bite this pink tube, he thought.

"Stand on the **bow**," Dad said. "You need to see the shark before it sees you. Watch for a long dark shape. Then **cast** your line."

Suddenly Dad threw his **lure** into the water.

A sleek body swam by and disappeared to the left.

"Scared him," Dad said. "Sharks don't see well, Jack. So drop your lure right by its nose."

Jack watched the water. When he started to cast, Dad stopped him. "That's a barracuda. Today, we're after sharks. Hey! Here comes one. It's yours, Jack. Cast!"

Jack's lure splashed like a pink snake in the water. The shark swam gracefully away.

And that's how the fishing went all morning. Sharks swam by. But then they swam away. But Jack did see a sea turtle and a stingray.

Around noon, another shark appeared. Jack aimed carefully. *Kerplunk!* The lure landed at the shark's nose.

The shark grabbed the lure and swam off. Dad hit the throttle and gave chase. Shark, boat, and fishermen sped across the flats.

"Keep your rod tip up!" Dad ordered. "Reel in the slack! Raise your rod again!"

Jack followed orders. Line screamed from the reel. The shark headed toward the **horizon**.

Jack's arms ached. But he forced the rod tip up. He rested the end of the rod on his stomach. Wow! Pain! Sweat stung his eyes. Blisters formed on his hands.

Dad shouted again. "He's tiring! Rod tip up! Bring him to the side. Don't let him dart under the boat. He'll cut the line!"

Chapter **3**

Would You Look at That!

Dad stopped the boat and took the rod. He pulled the shark close to the boat.

Jack dropped to his knees. He rested his forearms on the **gunwale**. He eyed the shark. The shark eyed him.

17

"Would you look at that, Dad!" Jack exclaimed. "How fast can they travel?"

"They usually swim about 6 knots per hour," Dad said. "This one did at least 40 knots per hour."

A *knot* equals about 6,076 feet.
A mile is 5,280 feet.

The shark was as long as Jack was tall.

Cautiously, Jack touched its sharp, pointed scales. The shark's gray, leathery skin felt like sandpaper.

"It's a nurse shark," Dad said. "They live on the sea bottom near shore."

"I can see its teeth," Jack said. "They're shaped like triangles."

"Right," Dad said. "Sharks were the first **vertebrates** to have fully developed jaws. Their teeth are on a sort of conveyor belt. Losing a tooth is no big deal. Another moves forward to replace it."

"This one looks pretty fierce," Jack said.

"Keep a safe distance," Dad reminded him. "Did you know that sharks must swim constantly? They don't have **swim bladders** like other fish. If they stop swimming, they sink."

"What'll we do with this one?" Jack asked.

"First, get a snapshot," Dad said. "I've been trained how to tag and release sharks. But we need to act quickly. We can't keep it out of water too long."

Jack reached for his camera. "What a shot this will make! Wait till I show the kids at school! Dad, I liked seeing this shark swimming free. I'm glad you aren't going to make shark stew."

"I don't kill sharks," Dad said. "Later this summer, I'm going to the Bahama Islands. There's a shark research station on Bimini. I'll help scientists tag and track sharks. But now we need to release this fellow."

"How much do you think it weighs?" Jack asked.

"Maybe over a hundred pounds," Dad said. He brought out a dart gun and a yellow tag. "I'll attach the tag. It goes on the base of the **dorsal fin**. He won't even feel it."

The shark hardly moved.

"The tag has a Bimini address," Dad added. "Anyone finding this shark can contact Bimini scientists. Tagging sharks helps them learn more about sharks."

Dad removed the tube lure from the shark. The shark lashed its tail. At first, it didn't swim away. Jack eased back.

What if it jumps into the boat? he thought.

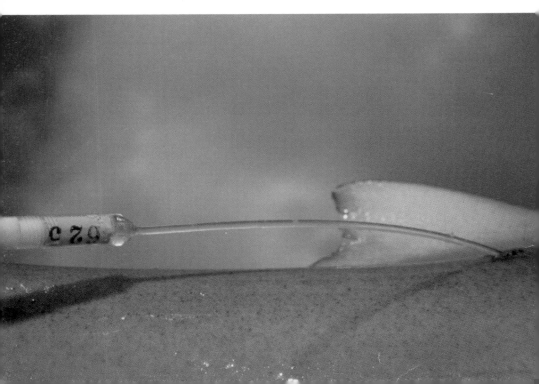

Chapter 4

Tag and Release

At first, the shark lay still as death. Then
suddenly, it swished its tail and splashed away.
Again Jack tasted salt spray. Dad replaced
their rods in the case.

"Enough fishing for today," he said. "Do those blisters on your hands hurt?"

"No," Jack said. They stung, but he wouldn't complain. He could put medicine on them later.

"I'll always remember that shark, Dad. And I'll have a picture for my room. Have you tagged many sharks?"

"Only a few. I'm just starting," Dad said. "But my California friend has released over a thousand."

"Awesome!" Jack said.

"He enjoys tagging and releasing sharks," Dad said. "He's protecting sharks while there are still plenty of them. He thinks of the future. He wants his grandkids to enjoy sharks too."

"That *is* really thinking ahead," Jack said. He thought for minute. "Dad, do you think the sea will ever run out of sharks?"

"It could happen," Dad said. "Sharks produce fewer young than other fish. My friend catches mako sharks."

22

"Male makos don't mate until they're three years old and six feet long. Female makos don't mate until they're six years old and over eight feet long. Years pass before they have young."

"Do sharks lay eggs?" Jack asked.

"Some do," Dad answered. "But most sharks give birth. Young sharks are called *pups*."

e birth of a lemon shark

"How long do makos live?" Jack asked.

"About 20 years," Dad replied. "They only have about six litters. The litters are small. There may be only half a dozen pups."

Jack thought about that. Maybe there weren't as many sharks as people believed.

mako shark

"Dad, does your friend ever keep any sharks?" Jack asked.

"He has kept four sharks for food. That's out of the 1,000 that he has caught," Dad said. "He shares the meat with friends. And he has his own special 'keeping' rules."

"What sort of rules?" Jack asked. He rubbed the sore spot on his stomach where the rod had poked him.

"He keeps only males," Dad explained. "They must be six feet long and weigh over 100 pounds. He never keeps a shark unless his home freezer is empty. Simple rules. Right?"

"Right," Jack agreed. "But it's hard to imagine an ocean with no sharks."

"Jack," Dad said. "Do you remember Gramp's farm pond in Kansas?"

"Sure, Dad," Jack said. "What about it?" He couldn't imagine what the farm had to do with sharks.

The Farm Pond

"Sharks swam in Kansas millions of years ago," Dad explained. He headed the boat across the flats toward home.

"Sharks swam where Gramp's pond is today," Dad continued. "Scientists found shark fossils there. Of course, those oceans are gone

26

now. And so are the sharks. But it makes me think about the past. And the future. About man. And about sharks."

"I really liked to fish in Gramp's pond," Jack said. "We caught bass, crappies, and bluegills. And you used to fry them on the outdoor grill." Jack's mouth watered. He remembered those fish suppers well.

"That's right! You were six then," Dad said. "What happened when you were ten?"

"I couldn't catch any more fish," Jack said. "I tried different baits. But no fish would bite. Gramp said the pond was fished out."

"Do you know why that happened?" Dad asked.

"Gramp let too many friends fish in his pond," Jack answered. "Soon all the fish were gone. None were left to lay eggs and produce young.

"But Dad!" Jack continued. "That was a small pond. Surely it couldn't happen in an ocean."

"Why not? It could," Dad said. "And it may. People must take steps to prevent it. Saltwater fishermen see it happening. They already see a difference. Ten years ago, they saw many sharks. Today, they see very few."

"I'd like to know more about sharks," Jack said. "Maybe they really *are* misunderstood."

"They're not misunderstood," Dad said. "They're hardly *understood* at all."

Jack didn't speak for a moment. He was thinking. "Dad, I looked right into that shark's eye. He looked back at me. I think I was seeing a very intelligent creature."

 28

"I agree," Dad said. "Sharks have had to be smart to survive this long. It's too bad so many people fear them. People hate things they fear. And people kill things they hate."

"But sharks are dangerous," Jack said. "I saw those teeth!"

"The government issued a book to sailors," Dad said. "It told them how to survive in the sea. It said that people who knew most about sharks feared them the least. You'll learn more about sharks soon."

"How?" Jack asked.

"Your uncle wants you to visit him in Hawaii before school starts. He's concerned about the sharks there. He may tell you things you'd rather not hear."

Here Comes
the Boat

Uncle Bill met Jack's plane in Honolulu. Jack liked the sweet smell of **plumeria**. Coconut palms grew in Uncle Bill's yard. In the distance, the sea sparkled with sunshine.

"Today, let's go to the boat docks," Uncle Bill suggested. "I understand you're interested in sharks."

"Yes, but I think they're scary," Jack said.

"Sometimes they are," Uncle Bill agreed.

At the dock, Jack heard shouts and laughter. He smelled fish. And he smelled **diesel** fumes. People pushed, shoved, and stepped on his toes.

"Here comes the boat!" a man shouted.

Jack stood on a packing crate to see. A sailboat was approaching. The crowd rushed forward. People waved fists full of money. Uncle Bill put his arm around Jack's shoulders. Jack didn't mind at all.

"What's that hanging from the boat's **rigging**?" Jack asked. "It looks like somebody's laundry on a clothesline."

"Those are shark fins," Uncle Bill said. "The crew's had a good catch. That's their way of advertising. These people are eager to buy shark fins."

"It must be an important business," Jack said. He watched more men shove forward.

"It *is* an important business," his uncle replied. "The crew needs to earn a living. And shark fins sell for over 30 dollars a pound."

"Wow!" Jack exclaimed. "What are they used for?"

"Cooks make shark's fin soup," Uncle Bill said. "For thousands of years, Asians have loved that soup. They consider it a special treat. In Asia, shark fins bring over 200 dollars a pound."

"This dock must be 'Fin Central,'" Jack said. "Why are these people in such a hurry?"

"These are cash-only deals," Bill said. "First come, first served. Over 30 million dollars a year changes hands here."

 33

sword fish

"What kind of sharks do the crews fish for?" Jack asked.

"They're not fishing for sharks at all," his uncle explained. "They're after swordfish and tuna. They

tuna

blue shark

net blue sharks by accident. They keep them for their fins."

"How big are blues?" Jack asked.

"They're about 13 feet long," Uncle Bill said. "They weigh up to 400 pounds."

Just then, a burly man shoved Jack. Uncle Bill caught him before he fell.

"I don't think I like this business," Jack said.

"Let's get out of here," Uncle Bill said. "I hate the shark fin business too. But you need to know what's going on. I'll tell you more about it. Then I want you to tell others. People need to be aware."

 35

Chapter 7

The Story Behind the Catch

Jack and his uncle were sitting on the patio.
"Those boats arrive every day with shark
fins," Uncle Bill said. "But the crew has left
carcasses of dead sharks behind."

"They don't use the meat for food?" Jack asked.

"No," his uncle said. "There's little market for shark meat. Or shark skin. Or shark **cartilage**. The crew just slashes off the fins."

"I don't like the sound of that," Jack said.

"I don't either," Bill said. "They throw the rest of the body overboard. Sometimes the sharks are still alive. Then they drown. Or they bleed to death. Then they're eaten by other sharks."

Jack shook his head. "I hate even thinking about that."

"So do I," his uncle said. "It's a cruel practice. And it's wasteful. I think it should be stopped!"

Jack thought about the shark he and Dad had released. He thought about his Gramp's pond. And he thought about the dead sharks. "Aren't there laws against shark finning?" he asked.

 37

"Yes," Uncle Bill said. "It's banned in federal waters of the Atlantic Ocean. And United States **delegates** to international **fishery** organizations are against finning. Yet it's still allowed in the Pacific Ocean."

"That doesn't make much sense," Jack said.

"It's a huge problem," his uncle agreed. "People concerned with the environment want to solve it. But it's hard to make everyone happy."

"Someday the oceans may run out of sharks," Jack said.

"Shark finners laugh at that idea," Uncle Bill said. "So do the soup lovers. They say there's no shark shortage.

"But people concerned about the environment disagree. They say there shouldn't be a shark fishery."

"So what will happen?" Jack asked.

"Concerned people are talking about the problem," Uncle Bill said. "Little is known about the blue shark population. Officials are

trying to guess how many sharks are left. And they're trying to find other markets for shark products so fisherman don't throw the carcasses back in the water."

"It's hard to count fish in the sea," Jack said.

"I believe concerned people will find a way," Uncle Bill said. "Organizations protect sea turtles, manatees, dolphins, and alligators. They will find a way to protect sharks too."

"I hope they find a way before it's too late," Jack said. He leaned back in his chair. He remembered the shark he had caught. He thought about looking into its eye and how it had looked back at him.

What can I do to help sharks? Jack wondered. He would have to think about that.

Chapter

Shark Enemies

"Sharks have lots of enemies, don't they?" Jack asked.

"Yes, they do," his uncle answered. "Even though they're one of the largest fish in the food chain. Besides whales, humans are sharks' biggest enemy."

"But Dad says sharks are survivors," Jack said.

"He's right," Uncle Bill said. "Sharks haven't changed much from their ancestors. But in ways they are quite **complex**.

"Their senses quickly tell them when food is near," Bill continued. "Sharks can hear and smell it."

"But what if the food is far away?" Jack asked.

"Their sleek bodies allow them to swim fast," Uncle Bill said. "This helps them catch prey. It also helps them escape danger."

"I think people need to know more about sharks," Jack said. "I've learned a lot this week. But even so, sharks still frighten me."

"They scare people who fish for sport too," his uncle said. "They fear sharks. So they kill them **intentionally**. People who fish **commercially** sometimes kill sharks. But it's usually an accident."

"That's because their hooks and nets are meant for other fish. Right?" Jack asked.

"That's right," Uncle Bill said. "People call sharks man-eating machines. Shark movies have caused that."

"Right," Jack agreed. "Movies usually give people wrong ideas about sharks."

"So do TV specials," Uncle Bill said. "They add to the shark scare. Before filming, sharks are excited into a feeding **frenzy**. Viewers see them thrashing in blood-tinged water. And that's scary.

"It's no wonder people fear sharks," his uncle continued. "It's because they don't know the truth."

"What do you mean?" Jack asked.

"Sharks seldom attack people," Uncle Bill said. "At least they seldom attack them on purpose. A shark attacks things that look like food. Seen from below, a swimmer may look like a seal. Seals are a shark's favorite food. So it attacks."

Seen from below, this surfer looks like a sea lion.

Jack looked at his uncle. "Intentionally or accidentally. It doesn't make much difference once you're bitten."

"People should avoid shark-infested waters," Uncle Bill admitted. "It's important to obey beach signs that warn of sharks."

WARNING! SHARKS SIGHTED USE CAUTION!

"That makes sense," Jack said. "That would protect people. But how can these same people protect sharks?"

"Oil spills and chemicals in the water can kill sharks," Uncle Bill said. "Those things endanger all sea life. People can clean up their acts."

"And they can make laws to protect sharks," Jack added. "But those are adult jobs," Jack said. "Is there anything kids can do?"

"I have a book I'll send home with you. You can read it on the plane," his uncle said. "Maybe it'll give you some ideas about sharks. About how you can help save them."

Chapter 9

How Can People Help?

"Dad," Jack said. "I've been thinking a lot about sharks. And about humans. We're both at the top of our food chains. We both eat smaller creatures."

"That's true," Dad said.

"We enter the shark's world to swim," Jack said. "We need to take care. But sharks seldom attack people. When sharks enter our world, they face sure death."

"That's true," Dad said. "They are destroyed."

45

"And they're wasted," Jack said. "They're not used for anything good. I want to help protect sharks from humans."

"You've certainly had a change of heart," Dad smiled. "What happened?"

"Sharks are in danger," Jack said. "I think we need rules about shark fishing. Before we don't have any left."

"You're remembering the farm pond," Dad said.

"Yes," Jack replied. "And Uncle Bill taught me more about people and sharks. The oceans need sharks. Sharks help clean the water by eating dead creatures."

"Shark meat could help feed starving people," Dad said.

"And scientists may discover shark-related medicines. They might find a cure for cancer. Or heart disease," Jack said.

"That's right," Dad agreed. "New and

useful products might be made from shark oil. Also from shark cartilage. But how will you help protect sharks?"

"I'll start by making people aware of them," Jack said. "To help sharks, people must know they need help.

"I have to make speeches in class once school starts," Jack said.

"Yes," Dad said. "I heard you mention it. But I thought you planned to tell scary tales."

"I've changed my mind," Jack said. "I'll tell kids the good things we've talked about. I'll tell them how sharks are killed just for fins. And I'll tell them how cruel finning is. I'll make my classmates understand."

"Good idea," Dad said. "But do you really think kids can help?"

"We can write letters," Jack said. "We can start by writing to our mayor. Then to our state senators. We can write to our governor."

"Why, Dad," Jack continued, "we could even write to the president. Letters would show our awareness and concern."

"I'll donate some stamps," Dad said. "Sometimes public officials really listen to young people. School kids have something that makes adults listen. Use that charm to bring about something good."

"I will," Jack promised. "And by the way. When are we going shark fishing again?"

Shark Facts

Scientific Classification

Selachii. There are over 350 species.

Length

Whale sharks may measure 49 feet. Pigmy cat sharks could fit in the palm of your hand. Average-sized sharks measure about 5 feet.

Weight

This varies from several tons to a few ounces.

Color

Most are gray or brownish gray.

Features

Sharks are cold-blooded. They have streamlined bodies with two stiff dorsal fins and strong tails. They don't have eyelids. Gills make breathing possible.

 49

Sharks can only move forward. Forward motion causes water containing oxygen to pass over the gills. Their skeletons are made of cartilage rather than bone.

They are born with 24 teeth. Lost teeth are replaced within a day. They have excellent senses of smell and hearing but poor eyesight.

Family Life

Little is known about a shark's family life. They have survived over 400 million years. Sharks grow slowly and mature late. Females frequently wait two years between litters. Sharks mate and then part. More research is needed.

Some sharks lay eggs which are anchored to the sea bottom for several months before they hatch. Others grow young inside their bodies, giving birth to full grown pups. Still others produce eggs which hatch inside the female's body. When pups are born, they are capable of caring for themselves.

Habitat

They live in seas and oceans, especially in warm climates. Some may migrate into freshwater rivers. They are territorial and tend to stay within their own domain.

Food

Normal diet is fresh fish and sea creatures. They also eat dead and decaying fish. They avoid poisonous fish, such as sea cucumbers, Moses sole, and scorpion fish. They also avoid porcupine fish, which inflate in sharks' throats and cause choking. Sharks feed at dawn and dusk when prey may be less alert. They even eat indigestible objects if they look like prey. Such objects are vomited later.

Enemies

Whales, larger sharks, humans, and ignorance are their greatest enemies.

Friends

Scientists tag and release sharks so more may be learned about them. Some people make others aware of sharks and their problems. The Office of Naval Research studies sharks and their behavior.

Other friends are pilot fish and remoras. Both pilot fish and remoras feed off scraps from sharks' meals and from parasites growing on sharks' skins. Remoras attach themselves to the shark.

GLOSSARY

ancient	very old
bow	forward part of a boat
canal	artificial waterway
carcass	dead body
cartilage	flexible material, such as humans have in their noses and ears, in place of bone
cast	to throw
channel	deeper part of a harbor
commercially	having to do with the buying and selling of goods
complex	hard to understand
delegate	person who represents another
diesel	type of fuel
dorsal fin	fin on a fish's back
fishery	place for catching fish or taking other sea animals

 53

flat	site of shallow water found near deeper ocean depths
frenzy	wild excitement
gunwale	upper edge of a boat's side
horizon	point where the earth and sky seem to meet
intentionally	on purpose
jasmine	tall climbing plant that has fragrant flowers
lure	artificial bait
plumeria	Hawaiian tree from which lei flowers are taken
reputation	overall character by which one is judged
rigging	ropes used to manage sails on a sailboat
swim bladder	organ that inflates to keep fish afloat
trade wind	wind blowing almost constantly from one direction
vertebrate	animal with a backbone